Collins First Irish Dictionary

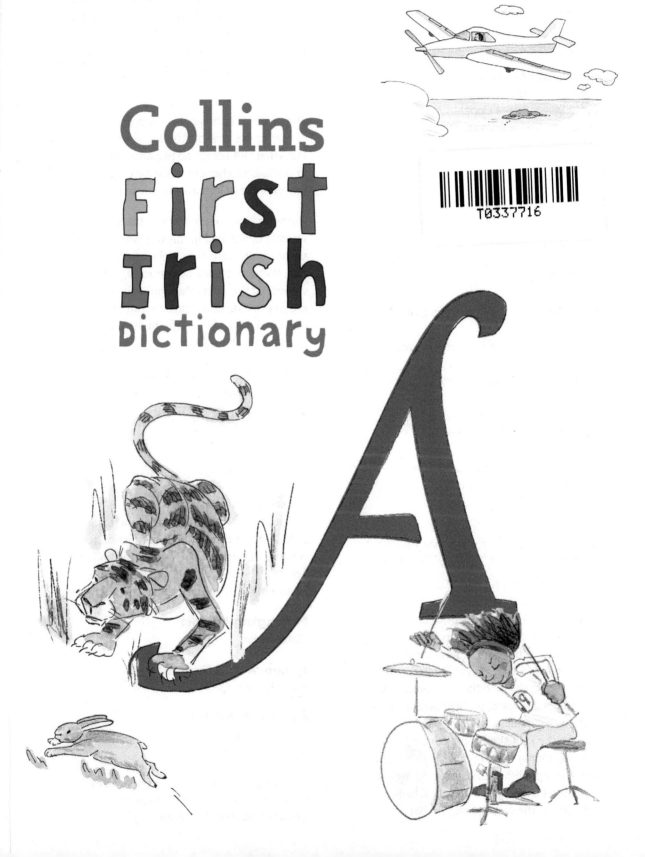

Published by Collins

An imprint of HarperCollins Publishers
Westerhill Road
Bishopbriggs
Glasgow G64 2QT

HarperCollins*Publishers*
Macken House
39/40 Mayor Street Upper
Dublin 1
D01 C9W8
Ireland

Third Edition 2021

Published as *Collins Very First Irish Dictionary*
2010, 2016

10 9 8 7 6 5

Text © HarperCollins Publishers 2010, 2016,
2021
Illustrations © Maria Herbert-Liew 2021

ISBN 978-0-00-842101-4

Typeset by QBS Learning

Printed and bound in the UK using 100%
Renewable Electricity at CPI Group (UK) Ltd

Acknowledgements

We would like to thank those authors and
publishers who kindly gave permission for
copyright material to be used in the Collins
Corpus. We would also like to thank Times
Newspapers Ltd for providing valuable data.

Managing Editor:
Maree Airlie

Artwork and Design:
Maria Herbert-Liew

For the Publisher:
Kerry Ferguson
Michelle I'Anson

**Audio pronunciation for every
Irish word and sentence at
collins.co.uk/homeworkhelp.**

Contents

How to use your dictionary

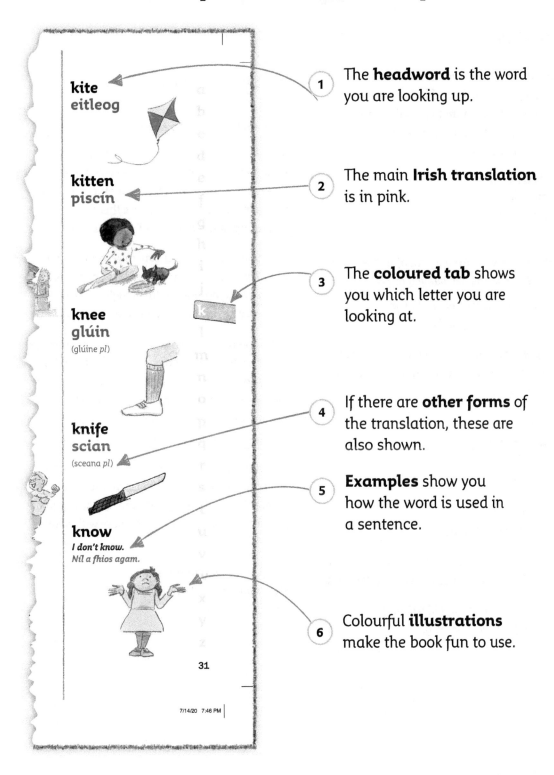

kite
eitleog

1 The **headword** is the word you are looking up.

kitten
piscín

2 The main **Irish translation** is in pink.

knee
glúin
(glúine *pl*)

3 The **coloured tab** shows you which letter you are looking at.

k

4 If there are **other forms** of the translation, these are also shown.

knife
scian
(sceana *pl*)

5 **Examples** show you how the word is used in a sentence.

know
I don't know.
Níl a fhios agam.

6 Colourful **illustrations** make the book fun to use.

31

7/14/20 7:46 PM

Word classes

Nouns

A **noun** is a word that is used for talking about a person or thing. **Nouns** are sometimes called "naming words" because they are often the names of people, places and things, for example:

> **man** *noun*
> **park** *noun*
> **bird** *noun*
> **computer** *noun*

Nouns are very often found after the words *a* and *the* or words like *our, my* or *his*.

We watched a <u>cartoon</u> on the <u>laptop</u>.
My <u>brother</u> is playing in the <u>park</u>.

Proper nouns are the names of people, places, days and months and <u>always</u> start with a capital letter.

> **Emma** *noun*
> **London** *noun*
> **Friday** *noun*
> **June** *noun*

<u>John</u> lives in <u>Glasgow</u>.
He went home on <u>Friday</u>.

When a **noun** is used with another word or words, this can be called a **noun phrase**.

She was wearing <u>a beautiful red dress</u>.
<u>All the children</u> were sleeping.

Some Irish nouns are:

gúna (meaning *dress*)
madra (meaning *dog*)

*Tá an **buidéal** folamh.*
(meaning *The bottle is empty*.)

In Irish, nouns can be *masculine (m)* or *feminine (f)*. This information is shown in the index. It is important to know whether a noun is masculine or feminine because this can affect the beginning of the noun itself after **an** *(the)*.

<u>Masculine</u> nouns do not generally change after **an** *(the)*. "The dress" is **an gúna**, and "the dog" is **an madra**. Be careful though, "the bird" is **an t-éan**, because **éan** begins with a vowel.

<u>Feminine</u> nouns mostly change their beginnings after **an** *(the)*. "Shoulder" is **gualainn**, but "the shoulder" is **an ghualainn**. However, feminine nouns beginning with a vowel do not change their first letter after **an**: "elbow" is **uillinn**, and "the elbow" is **an uillinn**.

The <u>plural</u> form of nouns (where there is more than one of something) sometimes looks quite different from the singular form. These <u>irregular</u> plurals are shown in the dictionary with *pl* after them.

bó (ba *pl*) (meaning *cow*)
The word for *the* changes in the plural too, so "the cows" is **na ba**.

Verbs

A **verb** is a word that you use for saying what someone or something does. **Verbs** are often called "doing words" because they talk about an action that someone or something is doing, for example:

> **eat** *verb*
> **cry** *verb*
> **talk** *verb*

Verbs are often found after nouns, or words like *she*, *they* or *it*.

The dog <u>barks</u> at the cat.
She <u>eats</u> sandwiches for lunch.

When you want to talk about something that you are doing right now (in the present), you use the **present tense** of the verb.

The children <u>are talking</u> to each other.
She <u>does</u> her homework before dinner.

When you want to talk about something that you did earlier (in the past), you use the **past tense** of the verb.

Anna <u>cried</u> when she fell off her bike.
The beetle <u>ran</u> across the floor.

You can make the **past tense** of many verbs by adding *d* or *ed* to the end of the verb, for example:

walk → walked
dance → danced

Sometimes you need to double the last letter before adding the *ed* ending in the **past tense**, for example:

stop → stopped
hug → hugged

Some verbs have a completely different way of making the **past tense**, for example:

go → went
sing → sang

Some Irish verbs are:

tabhair (meaning *give*)
faigh (meaning *find*)

<u>Tabhair</u> dom an leabhar, le do thoil.
(meaning *Give me the book, please.*)

Verbs in Irish usually come at the beginning of a sentence.

<u>Tá</u> an cat faoin tábla.
(meaning *The cat is under the table.*)

Adjectives

An **adjective** is a word that tells you more about a person or thing. **Adjectives** are often called "describing words" because they describe what something looks, feels, or smells like, for example:

big *adjective*
soft *adjective*
nice *adjective*

Adjectives are very often found before a noun, or after the verb *to be*.
She lives in a big house.
The caterpillar is long and green.

When you want to talk about something that is more than something else, you can use an **adjective** in different forms, usually ending in *er* or *est*.

bigger, biggest
soft, softer
nicer, nicest

I have the nicest sister in the world!
Yesterday was the wettest day of the year.

Some Irish adjectives are:

sona (meaning *happy*)
dubh (meaning *black*)

Tá sí sona.
(meaning *She's happy.*)

In Irish, adjectives go after the noun they are describing.

a black car
carr dubh

Adjectives in Irish can also change depending on whether the noun they describe is *masculine*, *feminine* or *plural*. The feminine form of Irish adjectives is shown in the Index on pages 75–80.

gúna *glan*
(meaning *a clean dress*)

léine ghlan
(meaning *a clean shirt*)

bróga glana
(meaning *clean shoes*)

Adverbs

An **adverb** is a word that tells you more about how someone does something, for example:

happily *adverb*
slowly *adverb*
well *adverb*

Adverbs are very often found after verbs, or sometimes before adjectives.

The snail moved slowly along the path.
The game was really exciting!

An example of an Irish adverb is:

go gasta (meaning *fast*)

Is féidir leo rith go gasta.
(meaning *They can run fast.*)

Colours
Dathanna

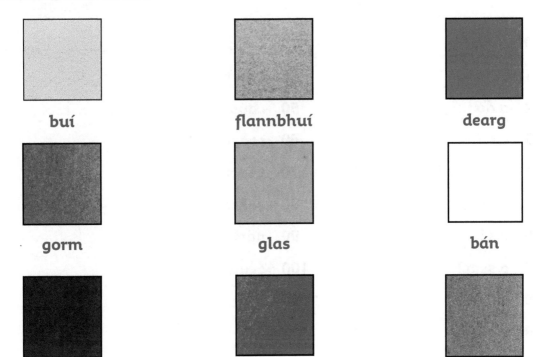

buí

flannbhuí

dearg

gorm

glas

bán

dubh

bándearg

liath

Shapes
Cruthanna

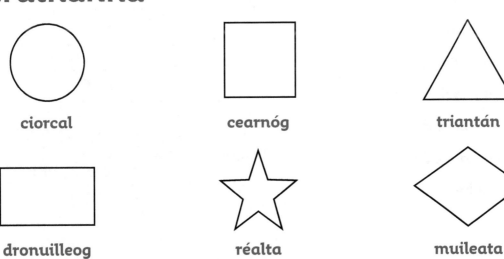

ciorcal

cearnóg

triantán

dronuilleog

réalta

muileata

Numbers
Uimhreacha

0	a náid	**30**	tríocha
1	a haon	**40**	daichead
2	a dó	**50**	caoga
3	a trí	**60**	seasca
4	a ceathair	**70**	seachtó
5	a cúig	**80**	ochtó
6	a sé	**90**	nócha
7	a seacht	**100**	céad
8	a hocht	**1000**	míle
9	a naoi		
10	a deich		
11	a haon déag		
12	a dó dhéag		
13	a trí déag		
14	a ceathair déag		
15	a cúig déag		
16	a sé déag		
17	a seacht déag		
18	a hocht déag		
19	a naoi déag		
20	fiche		

The days of the week
Laethanta na seachtaine

Monday	An Luan
Tuesday	An Mháirt
Wednesday	An Chéadaoin
Thursday	An Déardaoin
Friday	An Aoine
Saturday	An Satharn
Sunday	An Domhnach

The months of the year
Míonna na bliana

January	Eanáir
February	Feabhra
March	Márta
April	Aibreán
May	Bealtaine
June	Meitheamh
July	Iúil
August	Lúnasa
September	Meán Fómhair
October	Deireadh Fómhair
November	Samhain
December	Nollaig

Seasons
Na séasúir

spring
earrach

summer
samhradh

autumn
fómhar

winter
geimhreadh

The weather
An aimsir

It's cloudy. Tá sé scamallach.

It's hot. Tá sé te.

It's raining.
Tá sé ag cur
fearthainne.

It's windy. Tá sé gaofar.

It's snowing.
Tá sé ag cur
sneachta.

It's cold. Tá sé fuar.

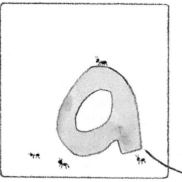

adult
duine fásta
(daoine fásta *pl*)

aeroplane
eitleán

after
i ndiaidh
after *lunch*
i ndiaidh *an lóin*

afternoon
tráthnóna
(tráthnónta *pl*)
at four o'clock
*in the **afternoon***
ar a ceathair a
*chlog **tráthnóna***

again
arís
*Try **again**!*
*Triail **arís** é!*

alphabet
aibítir

ambulance
otharcharr
(otharcharranna *pl*)

and
agus
*my cat **and** me*
*mise **agus** mo chat*

animal
ainmhí
(ainmhithe *pl*)

app
aip

apple
úll
(úlla *pl*)

arm
sciathán
(sciatháin *pl*)

ask
fiafraigh de
Ask *somebody.*
Fiafraigh de
dhuine éigin.

baby
leanbh
(leanaí pl)

bad
droch-
bad weather
drochaimsir

bag
mála

ball
liathróid

balloon
balún

banana
banana

basket
ciseán

bath
folcadán

beach
trá
(tránna pl)

bed
leaba
(leapacha pl)

bedroom
seomra leapa

before
roimh
before three o'clock
roimh a trí a chlog

bicycle
rothar

big
mór
*a **big** house*
*teach **mór***

bird
éan

birthday
breithlá
*Happy **birthday**!*
***Breithlá** sona!*

black
dubh
*a **black** dog*
*madra **dubh***

blanket
blaincéad

blue
gorm
*a **blue** dress*
*gúna **gorm***

boat
bád

body
corp

book
leabhar

boot
buatais

box
bosca

boy
gasúr

bread
arán

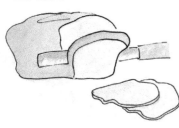

breakfast
bricfeasta

bridge
droichead

bring
tabhair

*Could you **bring** me a glass of water?*
***Tabhair** gloine uisce dom, le do thoil.*

brother
deartháir

(deartháireacha *pl*)

bucket
buicéad

burger
burgar

bus
bus

(busanna *pl*)

butter
im

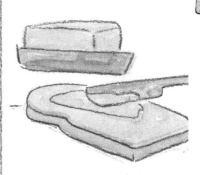

butterfly
féileacán

buy
ceannaigh

*She's **buying** fruit.*
*Tá sí **ag ceannach** torthaí.*

cake
cáca

calendar
féilire

call
glaoigh ar

Call this number.
Glaoigh ar an
uimhir seo.

candle
coinneal

(coinnle *pl*)

cap
caipín

car
carr

(carranna *pl*)

card
cárta

carrot
cairéad

castle
caisleán

cat
cat

caterpillar
bolb

chair
cathaoir

(cathaoireacha *pl*)

cheese
cáis

chicken
sicín

child
páiste

chips
sceallóga *pl*

chocolate
seacláid

chopsticks
cipíní
itheacháin *pl*

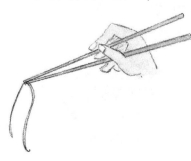

circle
ciorcal

circus
sorcas

classroom
seomra ranga

clean
glan

*a **clean** shirt*
*léine **ghlan***

clock
clog

clothes
éadaí *pl*

cloud
scamall

clown
fear grinn

(fir ghrinn *pl*)

coat
cóta

coffee
caife

cold
fuar

I'm **cold**.
*Tá mé **fuar**.*

come
tar

Come to me.
***Tar** chugam.*

computer
ríomhaire

cook

I can **cook**.
*Is féidir liom **cócaireacht**.*

costume
feisteas

count
áirigh

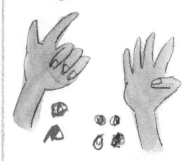

cow
bó

(ba *pl*)

cry
goil

*Why **are** you **crying**?*
*Cad chuige a bhfuil tú **ag gol**?*

cup
cupán

c

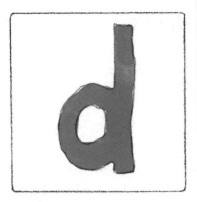

dad
daid
(daideanna *pl*)

dance
*I like **dancing**.*
*Is maith liom **bheith ag damhsa**.*

dangerous
contúirteach
*It's **dangerous**!*
*Tá sé **contúirteach**!*

daughter
iníon
(iníonacha *pl*)

day
lá
(laethanta *pl*)
*What **day** is it today?*
*Cén **lá** é inniu?*

dessert
milseog

dictionary
foclóir

difficult
deacair
*It's **difficult**.*
*Tá sé **deacair**.*

dinner
dinnéar

dinosaur
dineasár

dirty
salach
*My shoes are **dirty**.*
*Tá mo bhróga **salach**.*

do
déan
*What **are** you **doing**?*
*Cad **atá** tú **a dhéanamh**?*

doctor
dochtúir

dog
madra

doll
bábóg

dolphin
deilf
(deilfeanna *pl*)

door
doras
(doirse *pl*)

downstairs
thíos staighre
I'm downstairs!
Tá mé **thíos staighre**!

draw
tarraing

dream
brionglóid

dress
gúna

drink
ól
Drink *your water.*
Ól *do chuid uisce.*

drum
druma

duck
lacha
(lachain *pl*)

DVD
DVD
(DVDanna *pl*)

ear
cluas

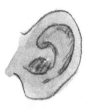

Earth
an Domhan

easy
furasta
*It's **easy**!*
*Tá sé **furasta**!*

eat
ith
*I eat a lot of **fruit**.*
*Ithim a lán **torthaí**.*

egg
ubh
(uibheacha *pl*)

elephant
eilifint

email
ríomhphost

empty
folamh
*The bottle is **empty**.*
*Tá an buidéal **folamh**.*

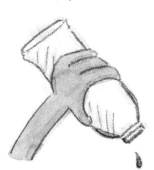

evening
tráthnóna
(tráthnónta *pl*)
*at six o'clock in the **evening***
*ar a sé a chlog **tráthnóna***

every
gach
*I brush my teeth **every** day.*
*Scuabaim mo chuid fiacla **gach** lá.*

exercise
cleachtadh
(cleachtaí *pl*)

eye
súil
(súile *pl*)

face
aghaidh
(aghaidheanna *pl*)

family
teaghlach

fast
go gasta
*They can run **fast**.*
*Is féidir leo rith **go gasta**.*

father
athair

favourite
*Pink is my **favourite** colour.*
*Bándearg an dath **is fearr liom**.*

feather
cleite

find
faigh
*I can't **find** my boots.*
*Ní féidir liom mo bhuataisí **a fháil**.*

finger
méar

fire
tine
(tinte *pl*)

fireworks
tinte ealaíne *pl*

first
céad
***first** prize*
*an **chéad** duais*

fish
iasc
(éisc *pl*)

floor
urlár
*Sit on the **floor**.*
*Suigh ar an **urlár**.*

flower
bláth
(bláthanna *pl*)

fly
cuileog

food
bia

football
peil

forest
foraois

fork
forc

fridge
cuisneoir

friend
cara
(cairde *pl*)

frog
frog
(froganna *pl*)

from
ó
*a letter **from** my friend*
*litir **ó** mo chara*

fruit
toradh
(torthaí *pl*)

full
lán
*The bottles are **full**.*
*Tá na buidéil **lán**.*

funny
greannmhar
*It's very **funny**.*
*Tá sé an-**ghreannmhar**.*

gate
geata

give
tabhair

Give me the book, please.
Tabhair dom an leabhar, le
do thoil.

game
cluiche

glass
gloine

giraffe
sioráf

garage
garáiste

glasses
spéaclaí *pl*

glove
miotóg

garden
gairdín

girl
cailín

glue
gliú

go
téigh
*Where are you **going**?*
*Cá bhfuil tú **ag dul**?*

goat
gabhar

goldfish
iasc órga
(éisc órga *pl*)

good
maith
*That's a **good** idea.*
*Sin smaoineamh **maith**.*

goodbye
slán

grapes
caora fíniúna *pl*

grass
féar

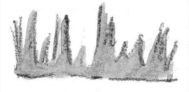

ground
talamh
*We sat on the **ground**.*
*Shuíomar ar an **talamh**.*

grow
fás
*Haven't you **grown**!*
*Nach tú a **d'fhás** ó shin!*

guinea pig
muc ghuine

guitar
giotár

a b c d e f **g** h i j k l m n o p q r s t u v w x y z

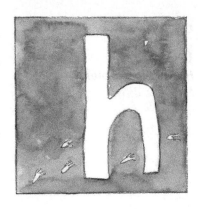

hair
gruaig
She's got black **hair**.
*Tá **gruaig** dhubh uirthi.*

hairdresser
gruagaire

hamster
hamstar

hand
lámh
(lámha *pl*)

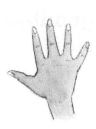

happy
sona
*She's **happy**.*
*Tá sí **sona**.*

hard
crua
*This cheese is very **hard**.*
*Tá an cháis seo an-**chrua**.*

hat
hata

have
*I **have** a bike.*
*Tá rothar **agam**.*

head
ceann
(cinn *pl*)

hear
cluin
*I can't **hear** you.*
*Ní **chluinim** thú.*

hedgehog
gráinneog

helicopter
héileacaptar

hello
Dia duit

a b c d e f g h i j k l m n o p q r s t u v w x y z

here
anseo
*I live **here**.*
*Tá mé i mo chónaí **anseo**.*

hide
*They**'re hiding** behind the tree.*
*Tá siad **i bhfolach** taobh thiar den chrann.*

holiday
saoire
*We're on **holiday**.*
*Táimid ar **saoire**.*

homework
obair bhaile

horse
capall

hospital
ospidéal

hot
te
*I'm **hot**.*
*Tá mé **te**.*

hour
uair an chloig
(uaireanta an chloig *pl*)

house
teach
(tithe *pl*)

hug
barróg

hungry
*I'm **hungry**.*
Tá ocras orm.

hurry up
déan deifir
***Hurry up**, children!*
***Déanaigí deifir**, a pháistí!*

ice cream
uachtar reoite

insect
feithid

internet
idirlíon

island
oileán

jacket
seaicéad

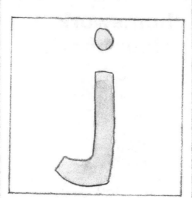

jam
subh

jeans
brístí géine pl

jigsaw
míreanna mearaí pl

job
jab

(jabanna pl)

juice
sú

Don't spill your juice!
Ná dóirt do chuid sú!

jump
léim

Jump!
Léim!

keep
coinnigh
*You can **keep** the book.*
*Tig leat an leabhar **a choinneáil.***

key
eochair
(eochracha *pl*)

kid
páiste

kind
cineálta
*a **kind** person*
*duine **cineálta***

king
rí
(ríthe *pl*)

kiss
póg
*Give me a **kiss**.*
*Tabhair dom **póg**.*

kitchen
cistin
(cistineacha *pl*)

kite
eitleog

kitten
piscín

knee
glúin
(glúine *pl*)

knife
scian
(sceana *pl*)

know
*I don't **know**.*
Níl a fhios agam.

lamp
lampa

learn
foghlaim

*I'm **learning** to dance.*
*Tá mé **ag foghlaim** damhsa.*

lady
bean
(mná *pl*)

laptop
ríomhaire glúine

leg
cos

lemon
líomóid

lake
loch
(lochanna *pl*)

late
mall

*I'm **late** for school.*
*Beidh mé **mall** ag an scoil.*

less
níos lú

*I've got **less** than him!*
*Tá **níos lú** agamsa ná aige!*

lamb
uan

laugh
déan gáire

*Why **are** you **laughing**?*
*Cad chuige a bhfuil tú **ag gáire**?*

letter
litir
(litreacha *pl*)

light
solas
(soilse *pl*)

like
I like cherries.
Is maith liom silíní.

lion
leon

listen
éist
Listen to me!
Éist liom!

little
beag
a **little** girl
*cailín **beag***

live
I live here.
Tá mé i mo chónaí anseo.

look
amharc
Look at the picture.
***Amharc** ar an bpictiúr.*

lorry
leoraí

lost
caillte
*I'm **lost**.*
*Tá mé **caillte**.*

loud
callánach
*It's too **loud**.*
*Tá sé ró**challánach**.*

love
I love you.
Mo ghrá thú.

lucky
You're lucky!
Tá an t-ádh ort!

lunch
lón
(lónta *pl*)

magician
draíodóir

make
déan

*I'm going to **make** a cake.*
Tá mé chun cáca a dhéanamh.

man
fear

(fir *pl*)

many
a lán

*There are **many** books!*
*Tá **a lán** leabhar ann!*

market
margadh

(margaí *pl*)

meal
béile

meat
feoil

medicine
cógas

meet
buail le

*I **met** my friend in town.*
Bhuail mé **le** mo chara sa bhaile mór.

mess
praiseach

milk
bainne

mobile
guthán póca

money
airgead

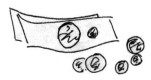

monkey
moncaí

month
mí

(míonna *pl*)
*What **month** is it?*
*Cén **mhí** é?*

moon
gealach

more
níos mó

*There are **more** girls than boys.*
*Tá **níos mó** cailíní ná*
buachaillí ann.

morning
maidin

(maidineacha *pl*)
*at seven o'clock in the **morning***
*ar a seacht a chlog **ar maidin***

mother
máthair

(máithreacha *pl*)

motorbike
gluaisrothar

mountain
sliabh

(sléibhte *pl*)

mouse
luchóg

mouth
béal

mum
mam

(mamanna *pl*)

music
ceol

name
ainm
(ainmneacha *pl*)

need
*I **need** a rubber.*
*Tá scriosán **uaim**.*

neighbour
comharsa
(comharsana *pl*)

new
nua

newspaper
nuachtán

next
*the **next** street on the left*
*an **chéad** sráid **eile** ar chlé*

nice
deas
*He's **nice**.*
*Tá sé **deas**.*

night
oíche
(oícheanta *pl*)

noise
callán

nose
srón

now
anois

number
uimhir
(uimhreacha *pl*)

nurse
altra

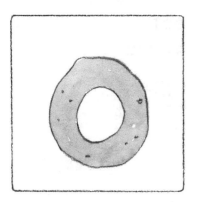

of
de
*a piece **of** cake*
*píosa **de** cháca*

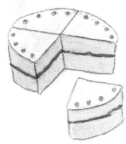

old
sean
*an **old** dog*
seanmhadra

open
oscail
*Why did you **open** the cage?*
*Cad chuige ar **oscail** tú an cás?*

orange
oráiste

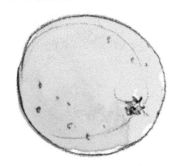

other
eile
*on the **other** side of the table*
*ar an taobh **eile** den tábla*

page
leathanach

paint
péinteáil
*I'm going to **paint** them blue.*
*Tá mé chun iad a **phéinteáil** gorm.*

paper
páipéar

parents
tuismitheoirí *pl*

peas
piseanna *pl*

pet
peata

park
páirc
(páirceanna *pl*)

pen
peann
(pinn *pl*)

phone
guthán

party
cóisir

pencil
peann luaidhe
(pinn luaidhe *pl*)

photo
grianghraf

pasta
pasta

people
daoine *pl*

piano
pianó
(pianónna *pl*)

picnic
picnic

picture
pictiúr

pirate
foghlaí mara

pizza
píotsa

plane
eitleán

plant
planda

play
imir

*I **play** tennis.*
Imrím leadóg.

playground
clós súgartha

(clóis súgartha *pl*)

pocket
póca

pocket money
airgead póca

police officer
póilín

pony
capaillín

postcard
cárta poist

potato
práta

present
bronntanas

pretty
gleoite
a pretty dress
gúna gleoite

prince
prionsa

princess
banphrionsa

puddle
slodán

puppet
puipéad

puppy
coileán

pushchair
bugaí linbh

pyjamas
pitseámaí *pl*

queen
banríon
(banríonacha *pl*)

quick
gasta
*a **quick** lunch*
*lón **gasta***

quiet
suaimhneach
*a **quiet** little town*
*baile beag **suaimhneach***

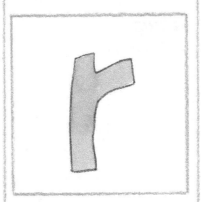

rabbit
coinín

race
rás

radio
raidió

rain
fearthainn

rainbow
tuar ceatha

read
léigh
*I **read** a lot.*
***Léim** cuid mhór.*

ready
réidh
*Breakfast is **ready**.*
*Tá an bricfeasta **réidh**.*

red
dearg
*a **red** jumper*
*geansaí **dearg***

restaurant
bialann

ribbon
ribín

rice
rís

rich
saibhir

*He's very **rich**.*
*Tá sé an-**saibhir**.*

right
ceart

*the **right** answer*
*an freagra **ceart***

ring
fáinne

river
abhainn

(aibhneacha *pl*)

road
bóthar

(bóithre *pl*)

robot
róbat

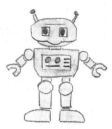

rocket
roicéad

room
seomra

run
rith

Run!
Rith!

sad
brónach
He's **sad**.
*Tá sé **brónach**.*

same
céanna
They're in the **same** class.
*Tá siad sa rang **céanna**.*

sand
gaineamh

sandwich
ceapaire

say
abair
*What **did** you **say**?*
*Cad a **dúirt** tú?*

scared
I'm **scared**.
Tá eagla orm.

school
scoil
(scoileanna *pl*)

scissors
siosúr *sg*

sea
farraige

second
dara

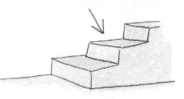

see
feic
I can **see** myself in the water.
***Feicim** mé féin san uisce.*

selfie
féinín

43

send
cuir
Send me an email.
Cuir ríomhphost chugam.

shadow
scáth
(scáthanna *pl*)

sheep
caora
(caoirigh *pl*)

shirt
léine
(léinte *pl*)

shoe
bróg

shop
siopa

shorts
bríste gearr *sg*

shout
béic
Don't shout!
Ná bígí ag béicíl!

show
taispeáin
Show me the photos.
Taispeáin na grianghraif dom.

shower
cithfholcadán

sick
tinn
She is sick.
Tá sí tinn.

sing
can
I love to sing.
Is breá liom bheith ag canadh.

sister
deirfiúr
(deirfiúracha *pl*)

sit
suigh
*Can I **sit** here?*
*An bhféadfainn **suí** anseo?*

skin
craiceann
(craicne *pl*)

skirt
sciorta

sky
spéir
(spéartha *pl*)

sleep
codail
*My cat **sleeps** in a box.*
Codlaíonn *mo chat i mbosca.*

slow
mall
*The tortoise is very **slow**.*
*Tá an toirtís an-**mhall**.*

smell
boladh
*Mmm, that **smells** good!*
*Mmm, tá **boladh** deas as sin!*

smile
miongháire

snail
seilide

snake
nathair
(nathracha *pl*)

snow
sneachta

snowman
fear sneachta
(fir shneachta *pl*)

soap
gallúnach

sock
stoca

sofa
tolg

son
mac

(mic *pl*)

sorry
I'm sorry!
Tá brón orm!

soup
anraith

space
spás

speak
*Do you **speak** Irish?*
***An bhfuil** Gaeilge **agat**?*

spider
damhán alla

spoon
spúnóg

sport
spórt

square
cearnóg

stairs
staighre

star
réalta

station
stáisiún

stick
greamaigh

Stick it onto the paper.
Greamaigh den pháipéar é.

sticker
greamán

stone
cloch

stop
stad

Stop, that's enough!
Stad, is leor sin!

story
scéal

(scéalta *pl*)

street
sráid

(sráideanna *pl*)

strong
láidir

She's very **strong**.
Tá sí an-**láidir**.

sun
grian

supermarket
ollmhargadh

(ollmhargaí *pl*)

surprise

What a surprise!
Cad mar iontas!

swim

I can swim.
Tá snámh agam.

swimming pool
linn snámha

(linnte snámha *pl*)

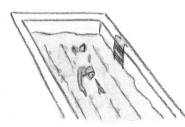

table
tábla

take
tóg
Take a card.
Tóg cárta.

talk
*You **talk** too much.*
Tá an iomarca cainte agat.

tall
ard
*a very **tall** building*
*foirgneamh an-**ard***

taxi
tacsaí

tea
tae

teddy bear
béirín

television
teilifís

text
*Can you **text** Lara?*
*An féidir leat **téacs a chur chuig** Lára?*

text message
teachtaireacht téacs

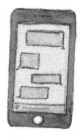

thank you
go raibh maith agat

think
smaoinigh
*What **are** you **thinking** about?*
*Cad air a bhfuil tú **ag smaoineamh**?*

third
tríú
*the **third** prize*
*an **tríú** duais*

tie
carbhat

tiger
tíogar

tired
I'm tired.
*I'm **tired**.*
Tá tuirse orm.

toast
tósta

today
inniu
*It's Monday **today**.*
Inniu an Luan.

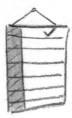

together
le chéile

toilet
leithreas

tomato
tráta

tomorrow
amárach
*See you **tomorrow**!*
*Feicfidh mé **amárach** thú!*

tooth
fiacail
(fiacla *pl*)

toothbrush
scuab fiacla

toothpaste
taos fiacla

tractor
tarracóir

triangle
triantán

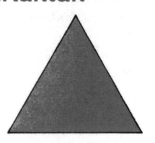

tortoise
toirtís

train
traein

(traenacha *pl*)

trousers
treabhsar

treasure
stór

towel
tuáille

T-shirt
T-léine

(T-léinte *pl*)

tree
crann

toy
bréagán

twin
leathchúpla

umbrella
scáth fearthainne
(scáthanna fearthainne *pl*)

uniform
éide

up
*The cat is **up** on the roof.*
*Tá an cat **in airde** ar an díon.*

upstairs
suas staighre

vanilla
fanaile
***vanilla** ice cream*
*uachtar reoite **fanaile***

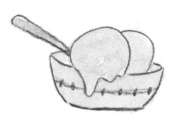

vegetable
glasra

very
an-
***very** small*
***an**-bheag*

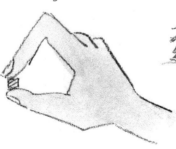

vet
tréidlia
(tréidlianna *pl*)

video game
físchluiche

visit
*We're going to **visit** the castle.*
*Táimid chun **cuairt a thabhairt** ar an gcaisleán.*

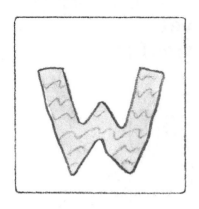

wait
fan
Wait for me!
Fan liomsa!

wake up
múscail
Wake up!
Múscail!

walk
siúil
He walks fast.
Siúlann sé go gasta.

wall
balla
There are posters on the wall.
Tá póstaeir ar an mballa.

want
Do you want some cake?
An bhfuil píosa cáca uait?

warm
te
warm water
uisce te

wash
nigh
Wash your hands!
Nigh do lámha!

watch
uaireadóir

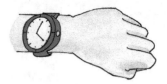

water
uisce

wave
tonn
(tonnta *pl*)

wear
caith
He's wearing a hat.
Tá sé ag caitheamh hata.

webcam
ceamara gréasáin

website
suíomh gréasáin
(suíomhanna gréasáin pl)

week
seachtain
(seachtainí pl)

*I play football every **week**.*
*Imrím peil gach **seachtain**.*

weekend
deireadh seachtaine
(deirí seachtaine pl)

*I go fishing at the **weekend**.*
*Téim ag iascaireacht ag an **deireadh seachtaine**.*

welcome
fáilte

well
go maith

*She played **well**.*
*D'imir sí **go maith**.*

wet
fliuch

wheelchair
cathaoir rothaí
(cathaoireacha rothaí pl)

white
bán

*I'm wearing a **white** shirt.*
*Léine **bhán** atá orm.*

wild
fiáin

*a **wild** animal*
*ainmhí **fiáin***

win
buaigh

*I always **win**.*
***Buaim** i gcónaí.*

wind
gaoth

window
fuinneog

winner
buaiteoir

with
le

*Come **with** me.*
*Tar **liomsa**.*

without
gan

***without** a coat*
***gan** chóta*

wolf
mac tíre

(mic thíre *pl*)

woman
bean

(mná *pl*)

word
focal

work
obair

*She **works** in a bank.*
*Tá sí **ag obair** i mbanc.*

world
domhan

write
scríobh

*I'm **writing** to my friend.*
*Tá mé **ag scríobh** chuig mo chara.*

wrong
mícheart

*That answer is **wrong**.*
*Tá an freagra sin **mícheart**.*

X-ray
x-gha
(x-ghathanna *pl*)

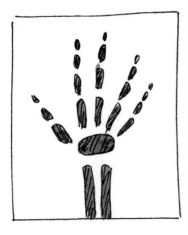

xylophone
xileafón

year
bliain
(blianta *pl*)
*I'm seven **years** old.*
Tá mé seacht
***mbliana** d'aois.*

yellow
buí

yesterday
inné
*I was late **yesterday**.*
*Bhí mé mall **inné**.*

young
óg
The children
*are **young**.*
Tá na
*páistí **óg**.*

zebra
séabra

zoo
zú
(zúnna *pl*)

Conversations
Comhráite

Please.
Le do thoil.

Hello!
Dia duit!

I'm fine, and you?
Tá mé go maith,
agus tú féin?

How are you?
Cad é mar atá tú?

Thank you.
Go raibh maith agat.

You're welcome.
Tá fáilte romhat.

What's your name?
Cén t-ainm atá ort?

My name's Eve.
Is mise Éabha.

Goodbye!
Slán!

Things I like to do
Rudaí is maith liom a dhéanamh

painting
péinteáil

watching TV
amharc ar an teilifís

dancing
bheith ag
damhsa

riding my bike
dul ag rothaíocht

playing games
físchluichí a imirt

singing
canadh

playing football
peil a imirt

reading
léamh

swimming
dul ag snámh

drawing
pictiúir a
tharraingt

The park
An pháirc

sandpit
poll gainimh

swing
luascán

climbing frame
fráma
dreapadóireachta

slide
sleamhnán

roundabout
timpeallán spraoi

The seaside
Cois farraige

sea
farraige

bucket and spade
buicéad agus
spád

crab
portán

starfish
crosóg mhara

gull
faoileán

rockpool
lochán carraige

sand
gaineamh

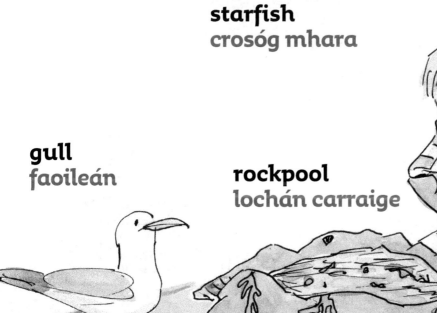

Vehicles
Feithiclí

tractor
tarracóir

plane
eitleán

fire engine
inneall dóiteáin

bike
rothar

motorbike
gluaisrothar

helicopter
héileacaptar

bus
bus

ambulance
otharcharr

car
carr

train
traein

63

Food and drink
Bia agus deoch

apple
úll

orange
oráiste

banana
banana

ice cream
uachtar reoite

cake
cáca

biscuits
brioscaí

juice
sú

milk
bainne

chocolate
seacláid

bread
arán

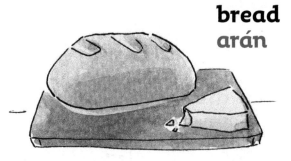

pizza
píotsa

cheese
cáis

sandwich
ceapaire

crisps
brioscáin phrátaí

chips
sceallóga

peas
piseanna

pasta
pasta

salad
sailéad

chicken
sicín

potatoes
prátaí

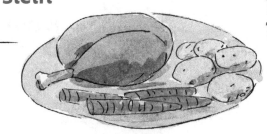

carrots
cairéid

Clothes
Éadaí

hat
hata

T-shirt
T-léine

dress
gúna

skirt
sciorta

shoes
bróga

trainers
bróga spóirt

gloves
miotóga

sweatshirt
léine
aclaíochta

coat
cóta

scarf
scaif

jeans
brístí
géine

socks
stocaí

Parts of the body
Baill bheatha

finger
méar

ear
cluas

eye
súil

arm
sciathán

tummy
bolg

hand
lámh

toe
ladhar

leg
cos

hair
gruaig

nose
srón

head
ceann

cheek
leiceann

mouth
béal

lip
liopa

knee
glúin

foot
cos

Family
Teaghlach

aunt
aintín

grandma
mamó

sister
deirfiúr

mum
mam

dad
daid

cousin
col ceathar

uncle
uncail

grandad
daideo

brother
deartháir

Animals
Ainmhithe

cat
cat

goldfish
iasc órga

hamster
hamstar

rabbit
coinín

dog
madra

budgie
budragár

chicken
sicín

donkey
asal

duck
lacha

horse
capall

cow
bó

sheep
caora

71

Wild animals
Ainmhithe fiáine

kangaroo
cangarú

monkey
moncaí

lion
leon

giraffe
sioráf

hippo
dobhareach

crocodile
crogall

snake
nathair

penguin
piongain

tiger
tíogar

elephant
eilifint

Mythical creatures
Ollphéisteanna miotasacha

alien
eachtrán

giant
fathach

ghost
taibhse

dragon
dragan

monster
ollphéist

fairy
sióg

unicorn
aonbheannach

mermaid
maighdean mhara

Irish-English Index

A, a

abair **say**

abhainn *f*
(aibhneacha) **river**

aghaidh *f*
(aghaidheanna)
face

agus **and**

aibítir *f* **alphabet**

ainm *m* (ainmneacha)
name

ainmhí *m*
(ainmhithe) **animal**

aip *f* **app**

airgead *m* **money**

airgead póca *m*
pocket money

áirigh **count**

a lán **many**

altra *m* **nurse**

amárach **tomorrow**

amharc **look**

an- **very**

an Domhan *m* **Earth**

anois **now**

anraith *m* **soup**

anseo **here**

arán *m* **bread**

ard **tall**

arís **again**

athair *m* **father**

B, b

bábóg *f* **doll**

bád *m* **boat**

bainne *m* **milk**

balla *m* **wall**

balún *m* **balloon**

bán, bhán **white**

banana *m* **banana**

banphrionsa *f*
princess

banríon *f*
(banríonacha)
queen

barróg *f* **hug**

beag, bheag **little**

béal *m* **mouth**

bean *f* (mná) **lady,
woman**

béic **shout**

béile *m* **meal**

béirín *m* **teddy bear**

bia *m* **food**

bialann *f*
restaurant

blaincéad *m*
blanket

bláth *m* (bláthanna)
flower

bliain *f* (blianta)
year

bó *f* (ba) **cow**

boladh *m* **smell**

bolb *m* **caterpillar**

bosca *m* **box**

bóthar *m* (bóithre)
road

bréagán *m* **toy**

breithlá *m* **birthday**

bricfeasta *m*
breakfast

brionglóid *f* **dream**

bríste gearr *sg*
shorts

brístí géine *pl* **jeans**

bróg *f* **shoe**

brónach, bhrónach
sad

bronntanas *m*
present

buaigh **win**

buail le **meet**

buaiteoir *m* **winner**

buatais *f* **boot**

bugaí linbh *m*
pushchair

buí, bhuí **yellow**

buicéad *m* **bucket**

burgar *m* **burger**

bus *m* (busanna) **bus**

C, c

cáca *m* **cake**

caife *m* **coffee**

cailín *m* **girl**

caillte **lost**

caipín *m* **cap**

cairéad *m* **carrot**

cáis *f* **cheese**

caisleán *m* **castle**

caith **wear**

callán *m* **noise**

callánach **loud**

can **sing**

caora *f* (caoirigh) **sheep**

caora fíniúna *pl* **grapes**

capaillín *m* **pony**

capall *m* **horse**

cara *m* (cairde) **friend**

carbhat *m* **tie**

carr *m* (carranna) **car**

cárta *m* **card**

cárta poist *m* **postcard**

cat *m* **cat**

cathaoir *f* (cathaoireacha) **chair**

cathaoir rothaí *f* (cathaoireacha rothaí) **wheelchair**

céad **first**

ceamara gréasáin *m* **webcam**

ceann *m* (cinn) **head**

céanna, chéanna **same**

ceannaigh **buy**

ceapaire *m* **sandwich**

cearnóg *f* **square**

ceart, cheart **right**

ceol *m* **music**

cineálta, chineálta **kind**

ciorcal *m* **circle**

cipíní itheacháin *pl* **chopsticks**

ciseán *m* **basket**

cistin *f* (cistineacha) **kitchen**

cithfholcadán *m* **shower**

cleachtadh *m* (cleachtaí) **exercise**

cleite *m* **feather**

cloch *f* **stone**

clog *m* **clock**

clós súgartha *m* (clóis súgartha) **playground**

cluas *f* **ear**

cluiche *m* **game**

cluin **hear**

codail **sleep**

cógas *m* **medicine**

coileán *m* **puppy**

coinín *m* **rabbit**

coinneal *f* (coinnle) **candle**

coinnigh **keep**

cóisir *f* **party**

comharsa *f* (comharsana) **neighbour**

contúirteach, chontúirteach **dangerous**

corp *m* **body**

cos *f* **leg**

cóta *m* **coat**

craiceann *m* (craicne) **skin**

crann *m* **tree**

crua, chrua **hard**

cuileog *f* **fly**

cuir **send**

cuisneoir *m* **fridge**

cupán *m* **cup**

D, d

daid *m* (daideanna) **dad**

damhán alla *m* **spider**

daoine *pl* **people**

dara **second**

de **of**

deacair, dheacair **difficult**

déan **do, make**

déan deifir **hurry up**

déan gáire **laugh**

dearg, dhearg **red**

deartháir *m* (deartháireacha) **brother**

deas, dheas **nice**

deilf *f* (deilfeanna) **dolphin**

deireadh seachtaine *m* (deirí seachtaine) **weekend**

deirfiúr *f* (deirfiúracha) **sister**

Dia duit **hello**

dineasár *m* **dinosaur**

dinnéar *m* **dinner**

dochtúir *m* **doctor**

domhan *m* **world**

doras *m* (doirse) **door**

draíodóir *m* **magician**

droch- **bad**

droichead *m* **bridge**

druma *m* **drum**

dubh, dhubh **black**

duine fásta *m* (daoine fásta) **adult**

DVD *m* (DVDanna) **DVD**

E, e

éadaí *pl* **clothes**

éan *m* **bird**

éide *f* **uniform**

eile **other**

eilifint *f* **elephant**

éist **listen**

eitleán *m* **aeroplane, plane**

eitleog *f* **kite**

eochair *f* (eochracha) **key**

F, f

faigh **find**

fáilte **welcome**

fáinne *m* **ring**

fan **wait**

fanaile **vanilla**

farraige *f* **sea**

fás **grow**

fear *m* (fir) **man**

féar *m* **grass**

fear grinn *m* (fir ghrinn) **clown**

fear sneachta *m* (fir shneachta) **snowman**

fearthainn *f* **rain**

feic **see**

féileacán *m* **butterfly**

féilire *m* **calendar**

féinín *m* **selfie**

feisteas *m* **costume**

feithid *f* **insect**

feoil *f* **meat**

fiacail *f* (fiacla) **tooth**

fiafraigh de **ask**

fiáin, fhiáin **wild**

físchluiche *m* **video game**

fliuch, fhliuch **wet**

focal *m* **word**

foclóir *m* **dictionary**

foghlaí mara *m* **pirate**

foghlaim **learn**

folamh, fholamh **empty**

folcadán *m* **bath**

foraois *f* **forest**

forc *m* **fork**

frog *m* (froganna) **frog**

fuar, fhuar **cold**

fuinneog *f* **window**

furasta, fhurasta **easy**

G, g

gabhar *m* **goat**

gach **every**

gaineamh *m* **sand**

gairdín *m* **garden**

gallúnach *f* **soap**

gan **without**

gaoth *f* **wind**

garáiste *m* **garage**

gasta, ghasta **quick**

gasúr *m* **boy**

gealach *f* **moon**

geata *m* **gate**

giotár *m* **guitar**

glan, ghlan **clean**

glaoigh ar **call**

glasra *m* **vegetable**

gleoite, ghleoite **pretty**

gliú *m* **glue**

gloine *f* **glass**

gluaisrothar *m* **motorbike**

glúin *f* (glúine) **knee**

go gasta **fast**

go maith **well**

go raibh maith agat **thank you**

goil **cry**

gorm, ghorm **blue**

gráinneog *f* **hedgehog**

greamaigh **stick**

greamán *m* **sticker**

greannmhar, ghreannmhar **funny**

grian *f* **sun**

grianghraf *m* **photo**

gruagaire *m* **hairdresser**

gruaig *f* **hair**

gúna *m* **dress**

guthán *m* **phone**

guthán póca *m* **mobile**

H, h

hamstar *m* **hamster**

hata *m* **hat**

héileacaptar *m* **helicopter**

I, i

i ndiaidh **after**

iasc *m* (éisc) **fish**

iasc órga *m* (éisc órga) **goldfish**

idirlíon *m* **internet**

im *m* **butter**

imir **play**

iníon *f* (iníonacha) **daughter**

inné **yesterday**

inniu **today**

ith **eat**

J, j

jab *m* (jabanna) **job**

L, l

lá *m* (laethanta) **day**

lacha *f* (lachain) **duck**

láidir **strong**

lámh *f* (lámha) **hand**

lampa *m* **lamp**

lán **full**

le **with**

le chéile **together**

leaba *f* (leapacha) **bed**

leabhar *m* **book**

leanbh *m* (leanaí) **baby**

leathanach *m* **page**

leathchúpla *m* **twin**

léigh **read**

léim **jump**

léine *f* (léinte) **shirt**

leithreas *m* **toilet**

leon *m* **lion**

leoraí *m* **lorry**

liathróid *f* **ball**

linn snámha *f* (linnte snámha) **swimming pool**

líomóid *f* **lemon**

litir *f* (litreacha) **letter**

loch *m* (lochanna) **lake**

lón *m* (lónta) **lunch**

luchóg *f* **mouse**

M, m

mac *m* (mic) **son**

mac tíre *m* (mic thíre) **wolf**

madra *m* **dog**

maidin *f* (maidineacha) **morning**

maith, mhaith **good**

mála *m* **bag**

mall, mhall **late, slow**

mam *f* (mamanna) **mum**

margadh *m* (margaí) **market**

máthair *f* (máithreacha) **mother**

méar *f* **finger**

mí *f* (míonna) **month**

mícheart, mhícheart **wrong**

milseog *f* **dessert**

miongháire *m* **smile**

miotóg *f* **glove**

míreanna mearaí *pl* **jigsaw**

moncaí *m* **monkey**

mór, mhór **big**

muc ghuine *f* **guinea pig**

múscail **wake up**

N, n

nathair *f* (nathracha) **snake**

nigh **wash**

níos lú **less**

níos mó **more**

nua **new**

nuachtán *m* **newspaper**

O, o

ó **from**

obair **work**

obair bhaile *f* **homework**

óg **young**

oíche *f* (oícheanta) **night**

oileán *m* **island**

ól **drink**

ollmhargadh *m* (ollmhargaí) **supermarket**

oráiste *m* **orange**

oscail **open**

ospidéal *m* **hospital**

otharcharr *m* (otharcharranna) **ambulance**

P, p

páipéar *m* **paper**

páirc *f* (páirceanna) **park**

páiste *m* **child, kid**

pasta *m* **pasta**

peann *m* (pinn) **pen**

peann luaidhe *m* (pinn luaidhe) **pencil**

peata *m* **pet**

peil *f* **football**

péinteáil **paint**

pianó *m* (pianónna) **piano**

picnic *f* **picnic**

pictiúr *m* **picture**

piscín *m* **kitten**

piseanna *pl* **peas**

pitseámaí *pl* **pyjamas**

píotsa *m* **pizza**

planda *m* **plant**

póca *m* **pocket**

póg *f* **kiss**

póilín *m* **police officer**

praiseach *f* **mess**

práta *m* **potato**

prionsa *m* **prince**

puipéad *m* **puppet**

R, r

raidió *m* **radio**

rás *m* **race**

réalta *f* **star**

réidh **ready**

rí *m* (ríthe) **king**

ribín *m* **ribbon**

ríomhaire *m* **computer**

ríomhaire glúine *m* **laptop**

ríomhphost *m* **email**

rís *f* **rice**

rith **run**

róbat *m* **robot**

roicéad *m* **rocket**

roimh **before**

rothar *m* **bicycle**

S, s

saibhir, shaibhir **rich**

salach, shalach **dirty**

saoire *f* **holiday**

scamall *m* **cloud**

scáth *m* (scáthanna) **shadow**

scáth fearthainne *m* (scáthanna fearthainne) **umbrella**

scéal *m* (scéalta) **story**

sceallóga *pl* **chips**

scian *f* (sceana) **knife**

sciathán *m* (sciatháin) **arm**

sciorta *m* **skirt**

scoil *f* (scoileanna) **school**

scríobh **write**

scuab fiacla *f* **toothbrush**

séabra *m* **zebra**

seachtain *f* (seachtainí) **week**

seacláid *f* **chocolate**

seaicéad *m* **jacket**

sean **old**

seilide *m* **snail**

seomra *m* **room**

seomra leapa *m* **bedroom**

seomra ranga *m* **classroom**

sicín *m* **chicken**

siopa *m* **shop**

sioráf *m* **giraffe**

siosúr *sg* **scissors**

siúil **walk**

slán **goodbye**

sliabh *m* (sléibhte) **mountain**

slodán *m* **puddle**

smaoinigh **think**

sneachta *m* **snow**
solas *m* (soilse) **light**
sona, shona **happy**
sorcas *m* **circus**
spás *m* **space**
spéaclaí *pl* **glasses**
spéir *f* (spéartha) **sky**
spórt *m* **sport**
spúnóg *f* **spoon**
sráid *f* (sráideanna)
  street
srón *f* **nose**
stad **stop**
staighre *m* **stairs**
stáisiún *m* **station**
stoca *m* **sock**
stór *m* (stórtha)
  treasure
sú *m* **juice**
suaimhneach,
  shuaimhneach
  quiet
suas staighre
  upstairs
subh *f* **jam**
suigh **sit**
súil *f* (súile) **eye**
suíomh gréasáin
  m (suíomhanna
  gréasáin) **website**

T, t
tabhair **bring, give**
tábla *m* **table**
tacsaí *m* **taxi**
tae *m* **tea**
taispeáin **show**

talamh *m* (tailte)
  ground
taos fiacla *m*
  toothpaste
tar **come**
tarracóir *m* **tractor**
tarraing **draw**
te, the **hot, warm**
teach *m* (tithe)
  house
teachtaireacht
  téacs *f* **text
  message**
teaghlach *m* **family**
téigh **go**
teilifís *f* **television**
thíos staighre
  downstairs
tine *f* (tinte) **fire**
tinn, thinn **sick**
tinte ealaíne *pl*
  fireworks
tíogar *m* **tiger**
T-léine *f* (T-léinte)
  T-shirt
tóg **take**
toirtís *f* **tortoise**
tolg *m* **sofa**
tonn *f* (tonnta) **wave**
toradh *m* (torthaí)
  fruit
tósta *m* **toast**
trá *f* (tránna) **beach**
traein *f* (traenacha)
  train
tráta *m* **tomato**

tráthnóna *m*
  (tráthnónta)
  afternoon, evening
treabhsar *m*
  trousers
tréidlia *m*
  (tréidlianna) **vet**
triantán *m* **triangle**
tríú **third**
tuáille *m* **towel**
tuar ceatha *m*
  rainbow
tuismitheoirí *pl*
  parents

U, u
uachtar reoite *m* **ice
  cream**
uair an chloig *f*
  (uaireanta an chloig)
  hour
uaireadóir *m* **watch**
uan *m* **lamb**
ubh *f* (uibheacha) **egg**
uimhir *f* (uimhreacha)
  number
uisce *m* **water**
úll *m* (úlla) **apple**
urlár *m* **floor**

X, x
x-gha *m*
  (x-ghathanna) **X-ray**
xileafón *m*
  xylophone

Z, z
zú *m* (zúnna) **zoo**